50 Best Potato Dishes

By: Kelly Johnson

Table of Contents

- Mashed Potatoes
- French Fries
- Baked Potatoes
- Potato Gratin
- Potato Wedges
- Hash Browns
- Potato Salad
- Scalloped Potatoes
- Potato Pancakes (Latkes)
- Roasted Potatoes
- Potato Soup
- Duchess Potatoes
- Gnocchi
- Patatas Bravas
- Potato Skins
- Tater Tots
- Hasselback Potatoes

- Potato Croquettes
- Loaded Baked Potatoes
- Colcannon
- Potato Au Gratin
- Smashed Potatoes
- German Potato Salad
- Sweet Potato Fries
- Shepherd's Pie
- Aloo Gobi
- Potato Curry
- Rösti
- Vichyssoise
- Bombay Potatoes
- Potato Pierogi
- Clapshot
- Potato Kugel
- Lyonnaise Potatoes
- Pommes Anna
- Potato Rosti

- Tater Tot Casserole
- Irish Boxty
- Potato Leek Soup
- Spanish Omelette (Tortilla Española)
- Potato Bread
- Potato Cheese Balls
- Potato Pizza
- Potato Scones
- Potato Cakes
- New Potato Salad
- Corned Beef and Potatoes
- Potato-Stuffed Peppers
- Coddle
- Twice-Baked Potatoes

Mashed Potatoes

Ingredients:

- 2 lbs russet potatoes, peeled and cubed
- 1/2 cup butter
- 3/4 cup whole milk or cream
- Salt and pepper

Instructions:

1. Boil potatoes in salted water until tender (15–20 mins).
2. Drain and mash.
3. Stir in butter and warm milk until smooth.
4. Season to taste.

French Fries

Ingredients:

- 4 large russet potatoes
- Oil for frying
- Salt

Instructions:

1. Peel (optional) and cut potatoes into thin sticks.
2. Soak in cold water 30 mins; dry thoroughly.
3. Fry at 325°F (160°C) for 5 mins; drain.
4. Increase oil to 375°F (190°C); fry again until golden.
5. Drain, salt, and serve.

Baked Potatoes

Ingredients:

- 4 large russet potatoes
- Olive oil
- Salt

Instructions:

1. Preheat oven to 425°F (220°C).
2. Scrub potatoes; prick with fork. Rub with oil and salt.
3. Bake directly on rack for 45–60 mins until tender.

Potato Gratin

Ingredients:

- 2 lbs Yukon Gold potatoes, thinly sliced
- 2 cups heavy cream
- 1 garlic clove
- 1 cup Gruyère cheese, grated
- Salt and pepper

Instructions:

1. Rub baking dish with garlic, then butter.
2. Layer potatoes, season, pour cream, and sprinkle cheese.
3. Repeat layers; bake at 375°F (190°C) for 50–60 mins.

Potato Wedges

Ingredients:

- 4 large potatoes
- 2 tbsp olive oil
- 1 tsp paprika
- 1/2 tsp garlic powder
- Salt and pepper

Instructions:

1. Cut potatoes into wedges.
2. Toss with oil and seasonings.
3. Bake at 425°F (220°C) for 30–35 mins, flipping halfway.

Hash Browns

Ingredients:

- 2 large russet potatoes, peeled
- 2 tbsp oil or butter
- Salt and pepper

Instructions:

1. Grate potatoes; rinse and squeeze dry.
2. Heat oil in skillet; press potatoes into pan.
3. Cook on medium until golden on both sides (about 5–7 mins per side).

Potato Salad

Ingredients:

- 2 lbs potatoes, boiled and cubed
- 1/2 cup mayonnaise
- 2 tbsp mustard
- 1/4 cup chopped celery
- 1/4 cup chopped red onion
- 2 boiled eggs, chopped (optional)
- Salt and pepper

Instructions:

1. Mix all ingredients gently.
2. Chill before serving.

Scalloped Potatoes

Ingredients:

- 2 lbs potatoes, thinly sliced
- 3 tbsp butter
- 3 tbsp flour
- 2 cups milk
- 1 cup shredded cheddar
- Salt and pepper

Instructions:

1. Make a roux with butter and flour; whisk in milk and cheese.
2. Layer potatoes in dish, pour sauce over.
3. Bake at 375°F (190°C) for 60–75 mins until tender and bubbly.

Potato Pancakes (Latkes)

Ingredients:

- 2 lbs potatoes, peeled and grated
- 1 small onion, grated
- 2 eggs
- 1/4 cup flour or matzo meal
- Salt and pepper
- Oil for frying

Instructions:

1. Grate potatoes and onion, then squeeze out excess moisture.
2. Mix with eggs, flour, salt, and pepper.
3. Heat oil in pan, drop spoonfuls of batter and flatten.
4. Fry until golden and crisp on both sides. Serve with sour cream or applesauce.

Roasted Potatoes

Ingredients:

- 2 lbs baby potatoes, halved
- 2 tbsp olive oil
- 1 tsp garlic powder
- 1 tsp rosemary or thyme
- Salt and pepper

Instructions:

1. Toss potatoes with oil and seasonings.
2. Spread on a baking sheet.
3. Roast at 425°F (220°C) for 35–40 minutes, flipping once.

Potato Soup

Ingredients:

- 2 lbs potatoes, peeled and diced
- 1 onion, chopped
- 2 cloves garlic, minced
- 4 cups chicken or vegetable broth
- 1 cup milk or cream
- Salt and pepper
- Toppings: bacon, chives, cheese

Instructions:

1. Sauté onion and garlic in butter. Add potatoes and broth.
2. Simmer until tender, about 20 minutes.
3. Blend part of the soup for creaminess, then stir in milk/cream.
4. Season and top as desired.

Duchess Potatoes

Ingredients:

- 2 lbs russet potatoes, boiled and mashed
- 4 tbsp butter
- 3 egg yolks
- Salt, pepper, nutmeg
- Optional: Parmesan cheese

Instructions:

1. Mash potatoes with butter, seasonings, and egg yolks.
2. Pipe into swirls on parchment-lined baking sheet.
3. Bake at 400°F (200°C) until golden (about 20 mins).

Gnocchi

Ingredients:

- 2 lbs potatoes, baked and mashed
- 1 ½ cups flour
- 1 egg
- Salt

Instructions:

1. Mix mashed potatoes, flour, egg, and salt into a soft dough.
2. Roll into ropes and cut into 1-inch pieces.
3. Boil in salted water until they float (2–3 mins).
4. Optional: pan-fry in butter for crispy texture.

Patatas Bravas *(Spanish-style spicy potatoes)*

Ingredients:

- 2 lbs potatoes, cubed
- Olive oil
- Salt
- For sauce: 1/2 cup tomato sauce, 1 tsp smoked paprika, 1/2 tsp cayenne, garlic, and vinegar

Instructions:

1. Roast or fry potatoes until crispy.
2. Simmer sauce ingredients and drizzle over potatoes.
3. Garnish with aioli, parsley.

Potato Skins

Ingredients:

- 4 large russet potatoes
- Olive oil
- Shredded cheddar
- Crumbled bacon
- Sour cream and chives

Instructions:

1. Bake potatoes at 400°F (200°C) for 1 hour.
2. Cut in half, scoop out centers, leaving a shell.
3. Brush with oil and bake again 10 mins.
4. Fill with cheese, bacon, and return to oven until melted.
5. Top with sour cream and chives.

Tater Tots

Ingredients:

- 2 cups cooked and grated russet potatoes
- 1 tbsp flour
- 1 tsp onion powder
- Salt and pepper
- Oil for frying

Instructions:

1. Mix ingredients and form into small cylinders.
2. Freeze 15 mins for firmness.
3. Fry at 375°F (190°C) until golden and crispy.

Hasselback Potatoes

Ingredients:

- 4 medium russet or Yukon Gold potatoes
- 3 tbsp melted butter or olive oil
- Salt and pepper
- Optional: garlic, herbs, cheese

Instructions:

1. Slice potatoes thinly without cutting all the way through.
2. Brush with butter/oil, season with salt and pepper.
3. Bake at 425°F (220°C) for 45–60 minutes, brushing with more butter halfway through.
4. Add cheese or herbs in final 10 mins if desired.

Potato Croquettes

Ingredients:

- 2 cups mashed potatoes
- 1/2 cup shredded cheese
- 1 egg
- Salt and pepper
- Bread crumbs
- Oil for frying

Instructions:

1. Mix potatoes, cheese, egg, and seasoning.
2. Shape into small logs or balls.
3. Roll in breadcrumbs.
4. Fry until golden and crispy, or bake at 400°F (200°C) until crisp.

Loaded Baked Potatoes

Ingredients:

- 4 large russet potatoes
- Shredded cheddar
- Cooked bacon bits
- Sour cream
- Chives
- Butter, salt

Instructions:

1. Bake potatoes at 425°F (220°C) for 45–60 mins.
2. Cut open and fluff with fork. Add butter, cheese, bacon, sour cream, and chives.

Colcannon *(Irish mashed potatoes with cabbage)*

Ingredients:

- 2 lbs potatoes, peeled and diced
- 1/2 head green cabbage or kale, chopped
- 1/2 cup milk
- 4 tbsp butter
- Salt and pepper

Instructions:

1. Boil potatoes until tender.
2. Sauté cabbage in butter until soft.
3. Mash potatoes with milk, mix in cabbage, season to taste.

Potato Au Gratin

Ingredients:

- 2 lbs thinly sliced potatoes
- 2 cups heavy cream
- 2 cloves garlic, minced
- 1 ½ cups Gruyère or cheddar cheese
- Salt and pepper

Instructions:

1. Layer potatoes in a buttered baking dish.
2. Mix cream, garlic, salt, pepper and pour over.
3. Top with cheese and bake at 375°F (190°C) for 1 hour or until bubbly and golden.

Smashed Potatoes

Ingredients:

- 1 ½ lbs baby potatoes
- Olive oil
- Salt, pepper, garlic powder, herbs

Instructions:

1. Boil potatoes until fork-tender.
2. Place on baking sheet, smash with glass.
3. Drizzle with oil, season.
4. Bake at 425°F (220°C) for 20–25 mins until crispy.

German Potato Salad

Ingredients:

- 2 lbs red potatoes, boiled and sliced
- 6 slices bacon
- 1/2 cup chopped onion
- 1/4 cup apple cider vinegar
- 2 tbsp sugar
- 1 tbsp Dijon mustard
- Salt, pepper

Instructions:

1. Cook bacon, remove and crumble. Sauté onions in bacon fat.
2. Add vinegar, sugar, mustard to pan; simmer briefly.
3. Toss warm potatoes with dressing and bacon. Serve warm.

Sweet Potato Fries

Ingredients:

- 2 large sweet potatoes, cut into thin fries
- 2 tbsp olive oil
- 1 tsp paprika
- 1/2 tsp garlic powder
- Salt

Instructions:

1. Toss fries with oil and seasoning.
2. Spread in a single layer on baking sheet.
3. Bake at 425°F (220°C) for 25–30 minutes, flipping halfway.

Shepherd's Pie

Ingredients:

- 1 lb ground lamb or beef
- 1 onion, diced
- 2 cloves garlic, minced
- 1 cup peas and carrots
- 2 tbsp tomato paste
- 1 tbsp Worcestershire sauce
- 2 lbs mashed potatoes
- Salt and pepper

Instructions:

1. Sauté onion and garlic, add ground meat, cook through.
2. Stir in tomato paste, Worcestershire sauce, and vegetables.
3. Spread meat mixture in baking dish, top with mashed potatoes.
4. Bake at 400°F (200°C) for 25–30 mins until golden on top.

Aloo Gobi *(Indian potato & cauliflower curry)*

Ingredients:

- 2 cups potatoes, cubed
- 2 cups cauliflower florets
- 1 onion, chopped
- 2 tomatoes, chopped
- 1 tsp turmeric, cumin, and garam masala
- 1 tsp ginger-garlic paste
- Cilantro for garnish

Instructions:

1. Sauté onion, add ginger-garlic paste and spices.
2. Add potatoes and cook 5 mins.
3. Stir in tomatoes and cauliflower. Cover and simmer until tender.
4. Garnish with cilantro.

Potato Curry

Ingredients:

- 3 medium potatoes, peeled and cubed
- 1 onion, chopped
- 1 tsp curry powder or garam masala
- 1/2 tsp turmeric
- 1 cup coconut milk or tomato puree
- Salt and chili to taste

Instructions:

1. Sauté onion, add spices and stir well.
2. Add potatoes and coat with spice mixture.
3. Add coconut milk or tomato and simmer until tender.

Rösti *(Swiss crispy potato cakes)*

Ingredients:

- 2 lbs russet potatoes (parboiled and chilled)
- Salt and pepper
- 2–3 tbsp butter

Instructions:

1. Grate cold parboiled potatoes. Season.
2. Press into a hot buttered pan and cook over medium heat until golden, flip and repeat.
3. Serve as rounds or wedges.

Vichyssoise *(Cold creamy potato-leek soup)*

Ingredients:

- 2 tbsp butter
- 2 leeks, sliced (white part only)
- 3 potatoes, peeled and diced
- 4 cups chicken or vegetable stock
- 1 cup heavy cream
- Salt, pepper

Instructions:

1. Sauté leeks in butter. Add potatoes and broth. Simmer until tender.
2. Puree and stir in cream. Chill thoroughly. Serve cold with chives.

Bombay Potatoes

Ingredients:

- 2 lbs potatoes, boiled and cubed
- 1 tsp mustard seeds
- 1 tsp turmeric, cumin, coriander
- 1 tomato, chopped
- Fresh cilantro

Instructions:

1. Heat oil, add mustard seeds, then spices.
2. Add tomato and stir, then potatoes.
3. Sauté until coated and golden. Garnish with cilantro.

Potato Pierogi

Ingredients:

- Dough: 2 cups flour, 1 egg, 1/2 cup sour cream, pinch salt
- Filling: 2 cups mashed potatoes, 1 cup cheddar cheese
- Butter and onion for topping

Instructions:

1. Mix dough and rest 30 mins. Roll out and cut circles.
2. Add filling and seal.
3. Boil until they float. Sauté in butter with onions if desired.

Clapshot *(Scottish mashed potato & turnip)*

Ingredients:

- 2 cups potatoes, boiled
- 2 cups turnips (swede/rutabaga), boiled
- 2 tbsp butter
- Salt and pepper
- Chives or green onion

Instructions:

1. Mash potatoes and turnips together.
2. Mix in butter, season, and garnish with chives.

Potato Kugel *(Ashkenazi Jewish casserole)*

Ingredients:

- 2 lbs potatoes, grated
- 1 onion, grated
- 3 eggs
- 1/4 cup flour or matzo meal
- Salt, pepper
- Oil or schmaltz

Instructions:

1. Mix all ingredients. Pour into oiled baking dish.
2. Bake at 375°F (190°C) for 1 hour or until golden and set.

Lyonnaise Potatoes *(French-style sautéed potatoes with onions)*

Ingredients:

- 2 lbs potatoes, sliced and parboiled
- 2 onions, thinly sliced
- 3 tbsp butter
- Salt and pepper
- Fresh parsley

Instructions:

1. Sauté onions in butter until golden, set aside.
2. Sauté potatoes in butter until browned and crisp.
3. Return onions to the pan, mix and heat through.
4. Season and garnish with parsley.

Pommes Anna *(Classic French layered potato dish)*

Ingredients:

- 2 lbs russet potatoes, thinly sliced
- 4 tbsp melted butter
- Salt and pepper

Instructions:

1. Layer potato slices in a buttered oven-safe skillet, brushing each layer with butter and seasoning.
2. Cover with foil and bake at 425°F (220°C) for 45–60 mins.
3. Uncover, press down with a spatula, and broil for crisp top.
4. Slice like a cake to serve.

Potato Rösti

Ingredients:

- 1 ½ lbs potatoes, peeled and grated
- Salt, pepper
- 2 tbsp butter or oil

Instructions:

1. Rinse and squeeze out moisture from grated potatoes.
2. Season and form patties or one large disk.
3. Fry over medium heat until golden on both sides.

Tater Tot Casserole

Ingredients:

- 1 lb ground beef or turkey
- 1 can cream of mushroom soup
- 1 cup frozen peas/carrots
- 1 cup shredded cheese
- 1 bag frozen tater tots

Instructions:

1. Brown meat, mix with soup and veggies, spread in baking dish.
2. Top with cheese and tater tots.
3. Bake at 375°F (190°C) for 30–35 mins until tots are crisp.

Irish Boxty *(Potato pancake made with mashed and grated potatoes)*

Ingredients:

- 1 cup raw grated potato
- 1 cup mashed potato
- 1 cup flour
- 1 egg
- ½ cup milk
- Salt

Instructions:

1. Mix all ingredients into a thick batter.
2. Cook in buttered pan like pancakes until golden on both sides.
3. Serve with butter or savory toppings.

Potato Leek Soup

Ingredients:

- 3 leeks, white part sliced
- 2 tbsp butter
- 4 potatoes, diced
- 4 cups chicken or veggie broth
- 1 cup cream (optional)
- Salt, pepper

Instructions:

1. Sauté leeks in butter. Add potatoes and broth, simmer until soft.
2. Puree and add cream if desired.
3. Season to taste and serve warm.

Spanish Omelette (Tortilla Española)

Ingredients:

- 3 potatoes, thinly sliced
- 1 onion, sliced
- 6 eggs
- Olive oil
- Salt

Instructions:

1. Fry potatoes and onions in oil until soft. Drain.
2. Beat eggs and mix in potatoes/onions.
3. Cook in a nonstick pan over low heat, flip once.
4. Serve warm or at room temperature.

Potato Bread

Ingredients:

- 2 cups mashed potatoes
- 2 ½ cups flour
- 1 egg
- 2 tbsp butter
- 1 tsp baking powder
- Salt

Instructions:

1. Mix all ingredients into a soft dough.
2. Roll out and cook on a hot griddle or bake at 375°F (190°C) for 25–30 mins.
3. Serve with butter or jam.

Potato Cheese Balls

Ingredients:

- 2 cups mashed potatoes
- 1 cup shredded cheese
- Salt, pepper, herbs
- Bread crumbs
- Oil for frying

Instructions:

1. Mix potatoes with cheese and seasonings.
2. Shape into balls, roll in breadcrumbs.
3. Chill then deep-fry or bake until golden.

Potato Pizza

Ingredients:

- 1 pizza dough
- 2-3 small Yukon gold potatoes, thinly sliced
- Olive oil
- 1 tsp rosemary
- 1 cup mozzarella cheese
- Salt and pepper

Instructions:

1. Roll out dough and brush with olive oil.
2. Arrange thin potato slices on top, overlapping slightly.
3. Sprinkle with rosemary, salt, pepper, and cheese.
4. Bake at 475°F (245°C) for 12-15 mins until crust is golden.

Potato Scones *(Scottish tattie scones)*

Ingredients:

- 1 cup mashed potatoes
- ¾ cup flour
- 1 tbsp butter
- ½ tsp salt

Instructions:

1. Mix all ingredients into a soft dough.
2. Roll out and cut into triangles.
3. Cook on a hot, dry griddle or skillet until golden on both sides.
4. Serve warm with butter or alongside breakfast.

Potato Cakes

Ingredients:

- 2 cups mashed potatoes
- 1 egg
- ½ cup flour or breadcrumbs
- Salt, pepper, herbs
- Butter or oil for frying

Instructions:

1. Mix ingredients into a thick batter.
2. Shape into patties and fry over medium heat until crisp and golden.
3. Serve as a side or snack.

New Potato Salad *(Herby and fresh)*

Ingredients:

- 1½ lbs baby new potatoes, boiled and halved
- 2 tbsp olive oil
- 1 tbsp lemon juice or vinegar
- 2 tbsp chopped fresh herbs (dill, parsley, chives)
- Salt and pepper

Instructions:

1. While potatoes are warm, toss with oil, lemon juice, and herbs.
2. Season and serve warm or chilled.

Corned Beef and Potatoes

Ingredients:

- 2 cups cooked corned beef, chopped
- 3–4 potatoes, cubed
- 1 onion, diced
- 1 tbsp butter or oil
- Salt and pepper

Instructions:

1. Fry onion until soft, add potatoes and brown slightly.
2. Stir in corned beef and cook until everything is hot and crisp.
3. Serve with eggs or mustard on the side.

Potato-Stuffed Peppers

Ingredients:

- 4 bell peppers, tops cut off and seeded
- 2 cups mashed potatoes
- 1 cup shredded cheese
- ½ cup cooked veggies or bacon bits
- Salt, pepper

Instructions:

1. Mix stuffing ingredients and fill peppers.
2. Place in baking dish, cover with foil.
3. Bake at 375°F (190°C) for 25–30 mins. Uncover and bake 10 more mins.

Coddle *(Irish sausage and potato stew)*

Ingredients:

- 4 sausages, sliced
- 4 potatoes, peeled and thickly sliced
- 1 onion, sliced
- 2 cups chicken or beef broth
- Parsley, salt, pepper

Instructions:

1. Layer ingredients in a pot, seasoning each layer.
2. Pour over broth, cover and simmer on low for 1–1.5 hours.
3. Serve with soda bread.

Twice-Baked Potatoes

Ingredients:

- 4 large baking potatoes
- ½ cup sour cream
- ½ cup shredded cheese
- 2 tbsp butter
- Salt, pepper, green onions

Instructions:

1. Bake potatoes at 400°F (200°C) for 1 hour. Cool slightly.
2. Cut in half, scoop out flesh. Mash with other ingredients.
3. Refill skins, top with more cheese.
4. Bake again for 20 mins until golden and bubbly.

www.ingramcontent.com/pod-product-compliance
Lightning Source LLC
LaVergne TN
LVHW081323060526
838201LV00055B/2436